The
Newborn King

Published by
Lion Hudson Limited
Wilkinson House, Jordan Hill Business Park
Banbury Road, Oxford OX2 8DR, England
www.lionhudson.com

ISBN 978 0 7459 7863 5

First edition 2019

A catalogue record for this book is available from the British Library

Printed and bound in China, May 2019, LH54

The Newborn King

Retold by Sarah J. Dodd
Illustrated by Raffaella Ligi

LION
CHILDREN'S

MARY HUMMED AS she swept the floor. She was thinking about Joseph, the man she was going to marry.

All of a sudden, someone spoke. Mary jumped.

There was an angel in the corner of the room!

"You're going to have a baby," said the angel.

"Name him Jesus. He will be the Son of God, the new king the Jews have been waiting for."

Mary was amazed. How could she have a baby? She wasn't married yet. But sure enough, as the months passed, she grew big with a baby.

Joseph took care of her, even though he wasn't the baby's real father – God was!

Then came more surprising news. "The Roman emperor wants everyone to go to their home town to be counted," Joseph told her. "We have to go to Bethlehem."

"But it's almost time for the baby to be born!" said Mary.

"The donkey will carry you," said Joseph.

The journey to Bethlehem was long and bumpy.
By the time they got there, Mary was exhausted. She
was looking forward to a comfortable bed and some
food. But all the inns were full. There was nowhere
to stay.

At last, an innkeeper took pity on them.

"I have a stable," he said. "It could do with a clean,
but it's warm and dry."

Mary was glad to sit down on a pile of straw. The
baby came quickly after that, with a loud cry as it
gulped in air.

"It's a boy," said Mary, "just as the angel told us.
His name is Jesus."

She wrapped Jesus tenderly in strips of cloth.
She shooed the donkey away from the manger and
laid the baby in it.

Out in the fields, a group of shepherds huddled around
their fire. One was dozing; another two were
talking quietly.

Suddenly, the sky seemed to explode with
light. The shepherds screamed and hid
their faces.

There was an angel speaking to them!
"Don't be scared," said the angel.
"I have good news, which will bring joy
to all people, everywhere. The king that
God promised has been born at last, in
Bethlehem. He's lying in a manger, wrapped in strips
of cloth."

The sky grew even brighter as thousands more angels
appeared, singing for joy.

All at once, they were gone. Only the stars glimmered
silently in the darkness.

One of the shepherds jumped up. "What are we waiting for? Let's go to Bethlehem and see this baby!"

They each scooped up a lamb and raced off to the village. They hammered on doors, they called out in the streets, and at last, in a scruffy stable, they found Mary and Joseph gazing down at their baby, Jesus.

"What we saw was amazing!" gabbled the shepherds. "The angel said…"

They told Mary what had happened, the words tumbling off their tongues.

And Jesus slept on, smiling in his sleep as the echo of the angels' song still whispered on the air.

A while later at the palace in Jerusalem, a messenger
came to King Herod. The King scowled. "I don't want
any more visitors."

  "But they are wise men from the east. They are looking
for a new baby king."

  "There is no baby here," snarled Herod, "but I suppose
I must deal with them. You had better show them in."

The wise men looked tired and dusty, as though they had come a long way. But there was a look of excitement in their eyes.

"We have studied the stars for many years," they said. "A new, bright star has appeared. It means that the king the Jews have been waiting for has been born at last. Where is he? We want to worship him."

Herod was worried. He didn't want a new king taking his throne!

"Go and look for him, then come and tell me where to find him," said Herod. He frowned. "I'd like to worship him, too."

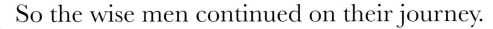 So the wise men continued on their journey. The star seemed to move across the sky, leading them onward. At last it stopped over Bethlehem.

The kings halted their camels. "That's the place," they said.

Sure enough, they went into the town and found Mary, Joseph, and Jesus.

They knelt down and unwrapped the gifts they had brought – strange things to give to a baby.

"I've brought gold," said one of the wise men, "because he is a king."

"I've brought frankincense," said another, opening a pot. "It burns with a scent that reminds us of God."

"And I've brought myrrh," said a third. "It's used to prepare bodies after death. There will be sadness and suffering in Jesus' life."

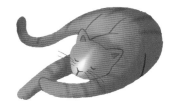

"What about King Herod?" the wise men said to each other. "Shouldn't we go and tell him the baby is here?"

"No!" One of the wise men spoke up. "I had a dream last night, and it warned me not to go back to Herod."

So the wise men climbed onto their camels and went back to their own country a different way.

After they had gone, Joseph had a dream, too. It was a very bad dream, in which an angel warned him that Herod was coming to harm Jesus.

Joseph got up, even though it was the middle of the night, and woke Mary.

"We must leave at once!" he said.

And the family fled through the darkness, to Egypt, where Jesus would be safe.

Other Christmas titles from Lion Children's Books

The Extra Special Baby, *Antonia Woodward*
On That Christmas Night, *Lois Rock – Alison Jay*
Jenny, the Shy Angel, *Anne Booth – Ruth Hearson*
The Pirate Christmas, *Suzy Senior –Andy Catling*